EARTHRISE

APOLLO 8 AND THE PHOTO THAT CHANGED THE WORLD

Written by
JAMES GLADSTONE

Illustrated by
CHRISTY LUNDY

Owlkids Books

For all of us down here on Earth.

With special thanks to everyone at OKB for getting this one off the ground so quickly — J.G.

Earthrise photo on page 32 and back cover courtesy NASA.

The author wishes to acknowledge the scholarship, enthusiasm, and support of Dr. Robert Poole, as well as the indispensable public archives of NASA's History Division.

Owlkids Books acknowledges the financial support of the Canada Council for the Arts, the Ontario Arts Council, the Government of Canada through the Canada Book Fund (CBF) and the Government of Ontario through the Ontario Media Development Corporation's Book Initiative for our publishing activities.

Published in Canada by
Owlkids Books Inc.
10 Lower Spadina Avenue
Toronto, ON M5V 2Z2

Published in the United States by
Owlkids Books Inc.
1700 Fourth Street
Berkeley, CA 94710

Library and Archives Canada Cataloguing in Publication

Gladstone, James, 1969-, author
    Earthrise : Apollo 8 and the photo that changed the world / written by James Gladstone ; illustrated by Christy Lundy.

ISBN 978-1-77147-316-3 (hardcover)

    1. Apollo 8 (Spacecraft)--Juvenile literature. 2. Earth (Planet)--Photographs from space--Juvenile literature. 3. Photographs--History--Juvenile literature. I. Lundy, Christy, illustrator II. Title.

QB637.G54 2018   j525.022'2   C2017-907851-8

Library of Congress Control Number: 2017963187

Edited by Karen Li
Designed by Alisa Baldwin

Manufactured in Dongguan, China, in April 2018, by Toppan Leefung Packaging & Printing (Dongguan) Co., Ltd.
Job #BAYDC55

A   B   C   D   E   F

ONTARIO ARTS COUNCIL
CONSEIL DES ARTS DE L'ONTARIO
an Ontario government agency
un organisme du gouvernement de l'Ontario

Canada Council
for the Arts

Conseil des Arts
du Canada

Canadä

OWL kids Publisher of Chirp, chickaDEE and OWL
www.owlkidsbooks.com | Owlkids Books is a division of Bayard CANADA

1968.

It was a year of unrest. Many nations were at war. People around the world marched for peace, fairness, freedom. They struggled to find the best way to live together.

Amid this conflict rose one shining moment, captured in a photograph—a picture that forever changed the way we saw ourselves and our world.

THE LIGHT WAS BREAKING

through clear open skies. It was a perfect morning for a launch.

The Saturn V rocket towered above the launchpad, the Apollo 8 spacecraft perched on top.

Three astronauts—Frank Borman, Jim Lovell, Bill Anders—walked toward the mighty metal ship that would whisk them far into outer space...

…farther than anyone had gone before.

The Apollo 8 crew was going to the Moon.

Cars clogged the roads, spilling over with anxious onlookers.

Millions of people listened in on radios.
They gathered around TVs.

Could human beings really reach the Moon?

What would they see when they got there?

There was sound like thunder—rumble and roar! The crowd stood their ground, while all the ground shook.

The Saturn V engines had burst into life!

We have liftoff!

Gracefully, powerfully, the rocket climbed...

higher...

faster...

out of sight, pushing Apollo 8 into Earth orbit...

...far above the crystal blue.

Soon the time came to break free from Earth orbit.
No one had ever done this before.

The engine fired again, setting Apollo 8 on course
for the Moon.

4, 3, 2, light on. Ignition.

Ignition.

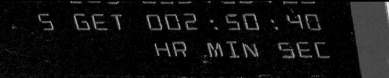

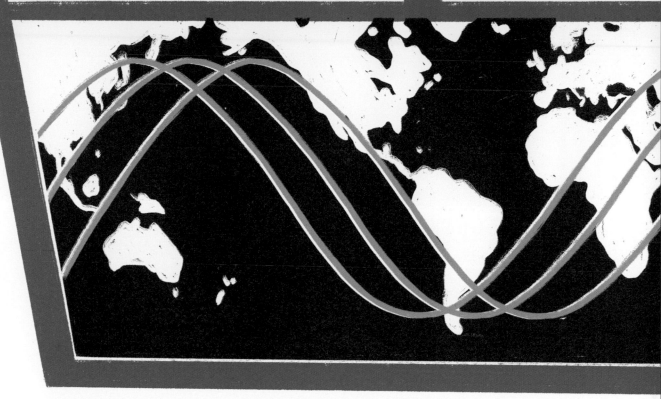

Mission control watched the spacecraft's speed on their screens.

The numbers got bigger as the rocket raced faster.

Then—just as planned—the Saturn V engine shut off
and broke away from Apollo 8.

Now the spacecraft was coasting on a human dream,
speeding the crew off to another world.

The farther they traveled the more awesome the view.

The astronauts saw the whole turning Earth—no countries, no borders—floating in the vastness of space.

Everyone they loved was on that tiny blue planet. And it was shrinking, getting smaller each time they looked.

On their third day out, the crew put on a show. They pointed a TV camera toward Earth. The picture all crackly, black and white, went out around the world.

You are looking at yourselves from 180,000 miles out...

Everyone who watched was amazed by this mysterious sight.

Soon after the broadcast, the astronauts arrived. The Moon came into view.

The spacecraft dipped into orbit, and the crew got to work taking pictures of the rocks and craters below.

Later, back on Earth, scientists would study those images, searching for the best sites to land future missions.

Once, twice, three times around the Moon, the crew's eyes were locked on the pocked and scarred lunar surface.

The fourth time around, they all looked up.

Earth—a soft swirl of color, an oasis of life—was rising above the lifeless rock of the Moon.

Anders captured what they saw in a photograph...

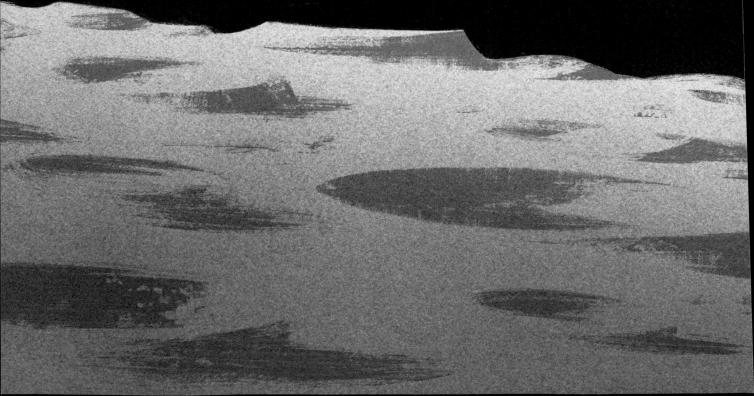

It was a picture of us all...

...to be remembered for all time.

THE PHOTO THAT CHANGED THE WORLD

The Apollo 8 mission was a huge moment in human history. Astronauts Frank Borman, Jim Lovell, and Bill Anders were the first people ever to see the whole, round Earth from space—the first people ever to fly to the Moon! And when the crew saw Earth rise above the Moon, Frank Borman described it as "the most beautiful, heart-catching sight" of his life.

The *Earthrise* photo captured that beauty for everyone back home who couldn't take that journey into space. But *Earthrise* showed us more.

Earthrise helped us to see our world for what it is: a planet without borders, a home to all peoples, a life-sustaining wanderer through space. This new vision of our world was so powerful that it inspired the first Earth Day, which we still celebrate today.

In a time when people still struggle to live together in peace, that picture of the rising Earth is as powerful now as it was in 1968. To the crew of Apollo 8, the *Earthrise* message was clear: Earth "really is one world."

What message does *Earthrise* send to you?

31901064681556